HOW TO B̲̅ ̲̅ ̲̅ ̲̅ ̲̅ ̲̅ ̲̅ ̲̅

AN INSTRUCTION MANUAL
FOR NEWBORNS

By Martin Baxendale

© Copyright Martin Baxendale 2008

Published by Silent But Deadly
Publications, 21 Bisley Road,
Stroud, Glos., GL5 1HF

Printed in England by
Stoate & Bishop Printers Ltd,
Shaftesbury Industrial Centre,
Cheltenham, Glos. GL51 9NH

All rights reserved. No part of this
book may be reproduced, stored in a
retrieval system or trasmitted in any
form or by any means, electronic,
mechanical, photocopying, recording
or otherwise, without the prior
permission of the publishers and
copyright holder.

ISBN: 978-0-9550500-7-7

DEAR NEW BABY,

So you've arrived at last! Whoopee! Now you're probably wondering what should be next on your to-do list.

Well don't worry. With the aid of this handy instruction manual, you'll always know <u>exactly</u> what to do in any situation you're likely to encounter as a New Baby.

From having your first feed and burping your first burp to taking your first steps and having your first fall, this invaluable manual will make sure that you're always ahead of the game.

And that's important in today's competitive go-getting world. You don't want to be left behind as all those other snotty-nosed New Babies out-perform you. No, you want to be out there leading the pack, achieving those goals, hitting those targets, filling those nappies.

MEET YOUR PARENTS

First, it's vital that you quickly identify and memorise these people's faces. They're your New Parents and your primary targets (look around you; they won't be far away. If in doubt, look for the most panic-stricken people in the room; that'll be them).

NOTE TO PARENTS OF NEW BABY: Glue photo of yourselves here (do not wear hats or sunglasses and do not try to disguise yourselves in any other way. Smiling is optional, but try not to yawn - even if you <u>have</u> been up all night trying to squeeze your New Baby out).

Your mission (should you agree to accept it) is to turn these New Parents into nervously twitching, sleep-deprived, brainless zombies. Good luck.

This message will self-destruct in ten seconds (only kidding; just chew it up when you get some teeth - see page 34).

Please note that (in most cases) one of your New Parents will be a 'Mummy' New Parent and the other a 'Daddy' New Parent.

They're quite easy to tell apart. For example, your designated 'Mummy' New Parent will have nice soft, round wobbly bits with which she can refuel and comfort you. Your 'Daddy' New Parent, on the other hand, will scratch you with his bristles and most likely drop you on your head. Treat them accordingly.

Nice soft, round, wobbly refuelling bits

Permanently tired eyes

Permanent yawn

Nice smiley face (when not yawning)

Usually nice long hair for pulling

YAWN!

'MUMMY' NEW PARENT

'DADDY' NEW PARENT

No soft, round wobbly refuelling bits

Tired eyes

Scratchy, stubbly grumpy-looking bits

Clumsy baby-dropping bits

Try not to get them mixed up. This can lead to confusion and disappointment, especially in the nice soft, round wobbly bits department. Latch onto your 'Daddy' New Parent by mistake and start sucking hard, and you're likely to be both disappointed and surprised when he drops you on your head in shock.

Should you ever need to identify one or both of them in a crowd, note that looking exhausted, yawning all the time and smelling of stale milk and nappies doesn't always mean someone is your New Parent. They're all like that. Look for ones that don't have a screaming New Baby attached and/or look like they're desperately trying to escape from you for a minute's peace and quiet.

7

RECOMMENDED OPERATING NOISE LEVELS

We strongly recommend maintaining your operating noise level at '<u>VERY LOUD</u>' throughout the day.

WAIL!!!

This is by far the most effective setting for holding the attention of your New Parents and keeping them by your side and constantly alert to your every little need.

Switch to '<u>QUIET</u>' mode for so much as a minute and before you know it they'll be sneaking off to have a lie down, make themselves a cup of tea, go to the toilet, and suchlike unnecessary distractions from their primary function and desire, which is to spend every minute of the day adoring you, doting on you and cooing over you. You're doing them a favour really.

But do watch out for the crafty use of <u>ear plugs</u> by your New Parents, especially at night-time.

Night, Night! We're going to bed now. Yell if you need anything.

Should you notice your New Parents sticking stuff in their ears (foam-rubber, cotton wool, socks) more than usual, we recommend cranking up your normal operating sound level from '<u>VERY LOUD</u>' to '<u>SONIC BOOM</u>', especially at your New Parents' so-called 'bedtime' (silly idea! Why would they want to sleep when they've got <u>you</u> to look at?)

If you don't have easy access to a decibel sound meter to check your operating sound levels are up to scratch, the following is a pretty good rule of thumb:

<u>Day-time operating noise levels</u>: Should be loud enough to annoy the neighbours three houses away.

<u>Night-time operating noise levels</u>: Should be loud enough to wake up the people three <u>streets</u> away.

SLEEPING

Sleep is for wimps, not for New Babies.

If you find you absolutely <u>must</u> sleep, we recommend you learn to <u>power</u> <u>nap</u> when your New Parents' backs are turned.

Better still, try to develop the ability to sleep with your <u>eyes</u> <u>open</u>. It's an ancient Oriental mystic trick that takes Yogic Masters years to perfect, but many New Babies get the hang of it in days (just don't tell all the New Parents).

SNORE!

But ideally try not to sleep at all - ever. This will leave you with much more free time during the day (and night) to practise your wailing.

Also, if your New Parents catch you napping, it'll only give them ideas about having a quick snooze themselves. Then they might miss you doing something really interesting and exciting, like blowing a snot-bubble with your nose.

And you know how much they love that sort of thing.

So why would they want to waste half the night sleeping when they could be getting in loads of extra cuddling, rocking, feeding, burping, dribble-mopping, nappy-changing, bottom-wiping and all that other stuff that New Parents can never get enough of?

It doesn't make sense.

WARNING: As much as your New Parents love spending every minute listening to you wailing, when the sleep-deprivation really kicks in, they might, in desperation, resort to hypnosis. Under no circumstances should you look at the swinging watch. Even if there's a picture of a clown on it.

Your eyelids are growing heavy ... you are
feeling sleepy ... very sleepy ... very, very
sleepy ... I am sleepy ... very sleepy ...
...my eyelids are growing heavy ...
.... I am going to sleep ...

REFUELLING

Now for the good stuff!!

<u>REFUELLING POINTS</u> A and B (remember these can only be found on your 'Mummy' New Parent).

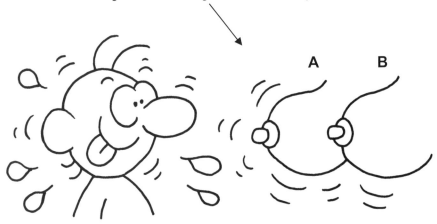

<u>WARNING</u>: Do <u>not</u> try to get them <u>both</u> in your mouth at the same time. That's just greedy, and not easy (though actually not impossible if you're really determined - oh what the hell, go for it!)

REFUELLING INSTRUCTIONS

This bit goes in…

…here

Not in here

And not up here

Do try to get it right. It's not rocket science.

And on behalf of agonised, screaming 'Mummy' New Parents everywhere, we'd like to point out that you should suck, not chew. That's <u>SUCK</u>!!! <u>NOT</u> <u>CHEW</u>!!!

17

Also, remember you're supposed to let go at some point. We know the milk and the boobies are nice, but do try to have some manners.

It's acceptable to show your appreciation by hanging on and not letting go when your 'Mummy' New Parent first tries to remove her refuelling point from your mouth.

You can even ignore the first few times she prods your cheek to get you to open up.

But if she starts hitting you on the head with a rolled up newspaper it's time to give up and let go, before the firemen arrive with the hydraulic spreading gear.

19

Alternative refuelling point C (see previous pages for insertion instructions).

NOTE: Alternative refuelling point C is not nearly as much fun. If you're offered the choice, we <u>strongly</u> recommend you go for A and B.

Here is where we introduce the first of your New Baby performance targets - for <u>weight gain</u>.

Your health visitor will call at regular intervals with your weight gain targets in grams and ounces per week. She'll be checking, so do your best to stick to the guidelines.

This is done by balancing your refuelling intake against your pooh output (see chart on page 25). If you don't gain enough weight, refuel more frequently and pooh less. Conversely, pooh more and refuel less to slow weight gain. It sounds complicated but you'll soon get the hang of it. Extra points for doing it without a spreadsheet.

<u>Weight gain target quick-checker diagram</u> :

WRONG!   RIGHT!   WRONG!

Weight gain after six months

<u>WARNING</u> : Eventually your New Parents will attempt to completely change your mealtime menu without consulting you. Resist this at all costs.

For a start, Sieved Broccoli and Carrot Cheesy Bake will not (usually) come out of your 'Mummy' New Parent's nice soft, round, wobbly, refuelling points but will arrive in <u>jars</u> and <u>bowls</u> and <u>on</u> <u>spoons</u>!

And <u>that</u> is a major change in your terms of employment as a New Baby, whereby you are contracted to provide your New Parents with ever-increasing quantities of pooh (see page 24) in exchange for regular refuelling via the 'Mummy' New Parent's nice soft, round, comforting wobbly bits.

You have every right to take industrial action by halting pooh production indefinitely until they reinstate your nice soft, round wobbly bits privileges. They'll soon cave in.

And in the meantime, anything offered to you from a jar, in a bowl or on a spoon is best not thought of as food, but as <u>ammunition</u>.

POOH PRODUCTION TARGETS

As a New Baby, the most important part of your job description is non-stop pooh production.

This is one area where you absolutely must <u>not</u> fall behind and fail to achieve your targets, because your New Parents are depending on you.

Sometimes their demands for more and more pooh can seem unreasonable - as fast as you fill the nappies, they whip them off and slap clean ones on you. It's an endless treadmill, but you mustn't let them down.

What exactly they <u>want</u> all that pooh for is anyone's guess, and probably best not to ask. It's just your job to keep it coming.

WEEKLY POOH PRODUCTION TARGETS CHART:

The following chart shows your weekly pooh production targets for your first three months.

Please note these are only the minimum requirements. If you can squeeze out more, all the better.

Etc.

Month 1   Month 2   Month 3

Note: These targets should be your average weekly pooh production across each month. Actual weekly production may fluctuate due to bouts of constipation and/or bouts of explosive tummy-bug squits.

You can of course use your first three months' weekly pooh production targets chart (see previous page) to calculate your pooh targets for future months.

For further months, just keep increasing the weekly amounts required on the same sliding scale until your New Parents run out of nappies and start using bin-bags.

NOTE: You're unlikely to ever produce more pooh than your New Parents can cope with, no matter how panic-stricken they may sometimes <u>appear</u>.

Indeed, they will eventually step up the pressure for <u>more</u> pooh by providing you with a bigger collecting receptacle and actively <u>encouraging</u> you to step up production, no matter how much you were previously coming up with.

Note limited-capacity nappy replaced with larger-capacity pooh collection vessel. They're heartless. But try your best to fill it.

If you worry that you might be falling behind with your pooh production quotas, stock-pile (under your mattress) a few jars of Strained Prunes And Custard, Sieved Cauliflower And Turnip, and Cheesy Sprout Purée.

If need be, that'll help you hit your end-of-month targets. In fact with that lot inside you, and no nappy on, you could probably hit anything that moves from 20 yards away.

But if you still find your pooh production is slowing down (perhaps due to a prolonged bout of constipation) it's a good idea to show willing by at least producing a few <u>smells</u> from time to time.

This will demonstrate that you're trying and that a new load of pooh might be on the way soon. Your New Parents will know you're making an effort and will appreciate that you're doing your best.

STOP THE SEX!!

Another very important part of your job as a New Baby is your role as the <u>sex police</u>. In short, it's your job to stop your New Parents having <u>any sex at all</u> for at least the first year after your birth.

People say that the best contraceptive is a New Baby, and they're right. No-one can really get in the mood when they're sleep-deprived and there's a New Baby wailing in the background, demanding to be picked up and cuddled.

Your New Parents are even less likely to get it on in the bedroom if every time they get into a clinch you manage to have a screaming fit, pooh yourself, throw up on your teddy, sneeze half a pint of snot down the front of your babygrow, get your dummy stuck up your nose and your head stuck in the bars of your cot - all at the same time.

Yes, that does all take a bit of planning and co-ordination, but the effect is worth it. They'll never leave you alone again, never mind trying to sneak off for a quickie. With any luck, they'll feel so guilty they'll never have sex again, ever.

BATH-TIME

The main point of bath-time is to get as much of the water as possible out of the bath and onto the floor and/or onto your New Parent(s) in the shortest possible time.

In between baths, practice your splashing technique in your cot and pram by thrashing around with your arms and legs, kicking off your duvet and throwing your teddy out.

The baby's learned how to **splash**!

And if you're in the <u>big</u> bath with 'Mummy' New Parent or 'Daddy' New Parent, you get extra points for managing to <u>pooh in the water</u>. And double-score if it's a really sloppy one that coats them like sea-birds in an oil-slick (hee-hee!)

33

TEETHING

Oh yes! You <u>will</u> get <u>teeth</u>!! Then it's pay-back time!! Old scores will be settled!! Past humiliations and neglect will be revenged!! Wa-ha-ha-ha-ha-!!!! Wa-ha-ha-ha-ha-h!!!!

Amazingly, New Parents <u>look forward</u> to your first tooth coming through and get all excited about it. The fools!!

Don't they <u>know</u> when you're teething you'll be even <u>more</u> grizzly, grumpy, grouchy, bad-tempered and inclined to scream and wail even <u>louder</u> and <u>longer</u>?!

And now you'll be <u>armed</u> as well!!

You have to pity the naive fools (and then gnaw all their stuff into soggy, chewed, unrecognisable lumps).

ESCAPING

All New Babies are of course naturally programmed to try to escape at every opportunity. In fact, it's your <u>duty</u> as a New Baby!

Here are some of the modes of escape that you can try, from your very first weeks onwards:

<u>WRIGGLING</u>: Good practice in the early days but not much real use - the best you can hope for is that your 'Daddy' New Parent might drop you on the floor.

<u>ROLLING</u>: Now you're talking. You can get around quite nicely by rolling. Once you've developed the knack, all you have to worry about is rolling <u>off</u> things as it's not always easy to see sudden drops coming up, like the edges of beds and settees.

<u>CRAWLING</u>: Better. Now you can see where you're going. The only problem is at first you'll find you tend to crawl <u>backwards</u> most of the time. So for a while the places you're trying to reach will keep getting further away, until you manage to get out of reverse gear.

Also, as soon as they realise you can crawl, your New Parents will stick you in a play pen. This is the point when you should think seriously about forming an escape committee.

STANDING UP AND FALLING OVER: You'll do a lot of this before you start walking. It can actually be quite a useful means of escape if you repeatedly stand up and fall over <u>in the same direction</u>.

Well done! Uh-oh! Well done! Uh-oh! Well done! Uh-oh....

Indeed, your New Parents will be so pleased that you're managing to stand up on your own, they'll actually <u>applaud</u> your efforts as you disappear towards the door.

39

WALKING: This is it! The real thing! Only bettered as a means of escaping from your New Parents by running and learning to drive a car.

The drawbacks:

1) You'll tend to bump into things a lot until your New Baby directional sat-nav kicks in properly. This is when bump cream starts to become a major household expense for your New Parents.

2) As soon as you start to walk, they'll slap the <u>reins</u> on you. This is when you realise that if you're going to make a break for freedom, you'll have to take one of the New Parents with you.

HAVING FUN

Of course it's not all hard work being a New Baby. You can have some fun too.

But you'll have to make your own entertainment. If you leave it to your New Parents, you'll be staring at a stupid clown mobile and listening to Baa, Baa Bloody Black Sheep all day long for the first few months. That or endless games of peek-a-boo (yawn!) and the terminally boring This Little Piggy Went To Market.

And later they'll try to persuade you that <u>sorting</u> <u>bloody</u> <u>shapes</u> for them is fun, fun, fun rather than work, work, work. Next they'll have you sewing sodding mailbags!

Of course you have to <u>pretend</u> to be amused. You don't want to hurt their feelings. But if you want some real fun, you'll have to come up with it yourself.

Here are just some of the many ways that New Babies have traditionally found to entertain <u>themselves</u>:

SPIT THE DUMMY: See how far you can spit your dummy. Extra points for trick shots (especially if they involve hitting your New Parents and/or unsuspecting domestic pets).

Double points for getting it to land somewhere that means they'll have to sterilise it before giving it back.

THROW THE TEDDY OUT OF THE PRAM: See how often they'll pick it up and give it back before losing their patience and stapling it to your mattress.

FIND THE POOH: When they're daft enough to leave you sitting unsupervised on the potty, see if they can find out where you poohed (anywhere but in the potty of course).

> I can smell it but I can't see it! You look behind the settee and I'll look inside our shoes!

> Warm ... cold ... warmer ...

> EMPTY!

WORD GAME: Your New Parents can't wait for the first time you say 'Mummy' or 'Daddy'. See just how much you can wind them up by repeatedly <u>sounding</u> like you're going to say 'Mummy' or 'Daddy' and then turning it into a totally different word.

Score 10 points for every word you come up with that <u>starts out</u> sounding like 'Mummy' and 'Daddy' but <u>isn't</u>.

EXTREME BABY SPORTS: And if you want something a bit more adrenalin-pumping, there are always the more extreme and dangerous Baby sports, like cat's-tail-pulling and stair-bouncing. Enjoy!

Did you close the **stair gate** when you came down?

BUMP!
BUMP!
BUMP!
BUMP!
BUMP!
BUMP!

NOTES TO MY FUTURE BABY BROTHERS AND SISTERS:

Make notes here (when you get some crayons and learn to scribble) of any personal New Baby experiences that you think might help your future baby brothers or sisters. Like your New Parents' weak points, insecurities and worst fears, and how best to wind them up, how to open the stair gate, where they hide the chocolate, etc (if you can't yet write, use diagrams).....

ALSO AVAILABLE (by Martin Baxendale) :

Over half a million copies sold in the UK and more than a million copies sold worldwide in over twenty languages.

YOUR NEW BABY

AN OWNER'S MANUAL

MODEL 1001A - GIRL
MODEL 1001B - BOY

Martin Baxendale's hugely popular spoof Baby Owner's Manual is available from bookshops and gift-shops throughout the UK.

An invaluable guide for all New Baby owners, explaining the many different operating modes, functions and features of the New Baby unit and how to look after it and maintain it. Guaranteed to ensure years of trouble-free operation, even for the most inexperienced of New Baby owners.

"I don't know what I would have done without your wonderful New Baby Owner's Manual. I had no idea how to work my New Baby properly and thought it was some sort of novel food-blender until I read your marvellous book (an unsolicited letter from a Mr A.N. Idiot of Milton Keynes).